Seven-time Winston Cup Champion Dale Earnhardt Sr,
referred to by many as "The Last True American
Cowboy," rides off into the sunset.

CREDITS
Publisher: Spurlock Photography, Inc.
Managing/Photo Editor: Brian Spurlock, Spurlock Photography, Inc
Editor: Jai Giffin, Host Communications, Inc.
Graphic Design: Dana Bart, Ashley Beavers, Dan Shute, Bob Slater, Kim Troxall and Craig Watkins, Host Communications, Inc.

Editorial Assistance: Mark Buerger
Photographers: Jim Brown, Jay Crihfield, Jai Giffin, Michael C. Hebert, Don Kelly, Joe Robbins, Brian Spurlock, Mark Terao
Production: Host Communications, Inc. • 904 North Broadway • Lexington, KY 40405 • (859) 226-4510

Orders for this magazine can be obtained by contacting:

Spurlock Photography, Inc.
10325 Lakeland Drive
Fishers, IN 46038
PH: 317-841-2857
Fax: 317-841-2868

The cover price of $9.99, plus $4.00 for postage/handling (Indiana residence add 5% sales tax). Payment can be made by money order, cashiers check or major credit card.

By Brian Spurlock

FOREVER A CHAMPION

Dale Earnhardt leads eventual winner Michael Waltrip in the 2001 Daytona 500.

©2001 JOE ROBBINS/
SPURLOCK PHOTOGRAPHY, INC.

©1996 BRIAN SPURLOCK

Growing up within walking distance of the Indianapolis Motor Speedway, I naturally love automobile racing. Fortunately, I have had the opportunity to photograph, up close, NASCAR, CART, Formula One and the IRL. Unfortunately, dangerous risks are always waiting around the corner. Dale Earnhardt's death at the 2001 Daytona 500 on the last turn on the last lap of the race has shocked the world.

Earnhardt certainly will be missed, but he will never be forgotten. The icon status of Elvis Presley and Princess Diana continue even today, and I think Dale's legacy and fan following will surpass these two if it hasn't already.

In this publication, I chose to dwell on the positive. There are more than 150 color photographs in the publication which celebrate a man who loved life, family and racing. I believe a picture is worth a thousand words and I have tried to let these photos convey Earnhardt's legendary status as a champion, but also give you a sense of his graciousness and kindness. His grin and smile will be with us forever.

The seven-time Winston Cup Champion seemed to never forget where he came from, and always seemed to relate with the common man. I remember being in the pits before the race at Talladega after it had rained. Drivers were standing in pit row waiting for the track to dry. Dale jokingly grabbed a towel and started wiping down the windshield of a security guard's motorbike. He seemed to get a kick out of being a famous person and helping out the common man.

My niece's friend tells the story of how she was lucky enough to get a parking pass for the infield at Bristol. After the race when leaving the infield, she had not locked her car door. Suddenly, Earnhardt opens the door, jumps in, and asks if he can get a ride across the track to a place he needs to be. Just imagine Dale Earnhardt jumping into your car after a race and needing a ride. Even though you can't take Dale in your car, at least the memories of him will forever be in your mind.

Earnhardt was the ambassador for NASCAR. He was a link from its past to the enormous success NASCAR is today.

Two of his last races were with his son at Daytona —The 24 Hours of Daytona and the Daytona 500. I think racing with Dale Jr. gave him even a greater enthusiasm to race. It's a shame that we can only speculate what the scene would have been in the Daytona 500 Victory Lane with Michael Waltrip and Dale Jr. finishing first and second in cars that Dale Sr. owned.

Dale Earnhardt Sr. is perhaps "America's last cowboy riding off into the sunset." At his funeral, the song "I'll Fly Away" was played, and this is how this publication ends. Dale Earnhardt Sr. will "Forever Be A Champion."

Special thanks to everyone at Host Communications for their time and effort in putting this publication together in such a timely manner. Special thanks to my attorney and father, Ben Spurlock, for his help in handling legal matters and contracts. Last, but not least, special thanks to my wife, Sally, for her support and love in putting this publication together.

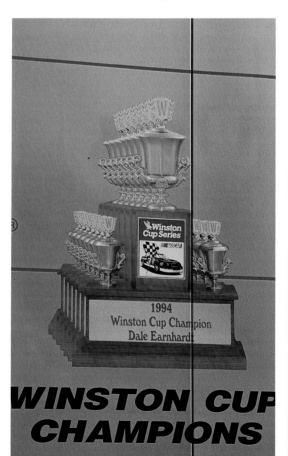

WINSTON CUP CHAMPIONS

1994
Winston Cup Champion
Dale Earnhardt

©1997 BRIAN SPURLOCK

©1997 BRIAN SPURLOCK

©2001 MARK TERAO/SPURLOCK PHOTOGRAPHY, INC.

Future orders for this publication can be made by contacting;

Spurlock Photography, Inc.
10325 Lakeland Drive
Fishers, Indiana 46038

Phone (317) 841-2857

Fax (317) 841-2868

Orders will also be taken online at: www.A-Dale-Earnhardt-photocollectible.com

The cost is $9.99, plus $4.00 for shipping and handling for a total of $13.99 (Indiana residents, please add 5% sales tax). Payable by money order, cashier's check, Visa or Mastercard. Please allow 2-3 weeks for delivery.

CAREER WINNING STATISTICS

DATE	SITE	START POS.	MONEY WON
1979			
April 1	Bristol	9	$19,800
1980			
March 16	Atlanta	31	$36,300
March 30	Bristol	4	$20,625
July 12	Nashville	7	$14,600
September 28	Martinsville	7	$25,375
October 5	Charlotte	4	$49,050
1982			
April 4	Darlington	5	$31,450
1983			
July 16	Nashville	3	$23,125
July 31	Talladega	4	$46,950
1984			
July 29	Talladega	3	$47,100
November 11	Atlanta	10	$40,610
1985			
February 24	Richmond	4	$33,625
April 6	Bristol	12	$31,525
August 24	Bristol	1	$34,675
September 22	Martinsville	11	$37,725
1986			
April 13	Darlington	4	$52,250
April 20	North Wilkesboro	5	$38,550
May 25	Charlotte	3	$98,150
October 5	Charlotte	3	$82,050
November 2	Atlanta	4	$67,950
1987			
March 1	Rockingham	14	$53,900
March 8	Richmond	3	$49,150
March 29	Darlington	2	$52,985
April 5	North Wilkesboro	3	$44,675
April 12	Bristol	3	$43,850
April 26	Martinsville	4	$50,850
June 28	Michigan	5	$60,250
July 19	Pocono	16	$55,875
August 22	Bristol	6	$47,175
September 6	Darlington	5	$64,650
September 13	Richmond	8	$44,950
1988			
March 20	Atlanta	2	$67,950
April 24	Martinsville	14	$53,550
August 27	Bristol	5	$48,500
1989			
April 16	North Wilkesboro	3	$51,225
June 4	Dover	2	$59,350
September 3	Darlington	10	$71,150
September 17	Dover	15	$59,950
November 19	Atlanta	3	$81,700

1990

March 18	Atlanta	1	$85,000
April 1	Darlington	15	$61,985
May 6	Talladega	5	$98,975
June 24	Michigan	5	$72,950
July 7	Daytona	3	$72,850
July 29	Talladega	1	$152,975
September 2	Darlington	1	$110,350
September 9	Richmond	6	$59,225
November 4	Phoenix	3	$72,100

1991

February 24	Richmond	19	$67,950
April 28	Martinsville	10	$63,600
July 28	Talladega	4	$88,670
September 29	North Wilkesboro	1	$69,350

1992

May 24	Charlotte	13	$125,100

1993

March 28	Darlington	1	$64,815
May 30	Charlotte	14	$156,650
June 6	Dover	8	$68,030
July 3	Daytona	5	$75,940
July 18	Pocono	11	$66,795
July 25	Talladega	11	$87,315

1994

March 27	Darlington	9	$70,190
April 10	Bristol	24	$72,570
May 1	Talladega	4	$94,865
October 23	Rockingham	20	$60,600

1995

April 9	North Wilkesboro	5	$77,400
May 7	Sears Point	4	$74,860
August 5	Indianapolis	13	$565,600
September 24	Martinsville	2	$78,150
November 12	Atlanta	11	$141,850

1996

February 25	Rockingham	18	$83,840
March 10	Atlanta	18	$91,050

1998

February 15	Daytona	4	$1,059,805

1999

April 25	Talladega	17	$147,795
August 28	Bristol	26	$89,880
October 17	Talladega	27	$120,290

2000

March 12	Atlanta	35	$123,100
October 15	Talladega	20	$135,900

TOTALS

Starts	Wins	Poles	Money Won
675	76	22	$41,411,551

Mirrored images of Dale Earnhardt will forever be etched in our minds.

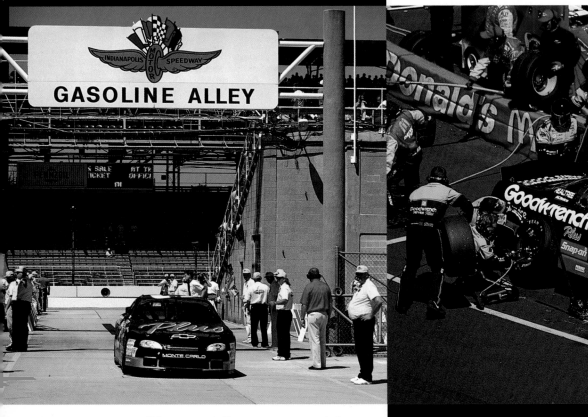

"The Flying Aces" speed into action for a pit stop at Martinsville.

The world's greatest drivers have entered Gasoline Alley for nearly a century.

Earnhardt salutes the fans on his victory lap at the Brickyard in 1995.
©1995 PHOTO BY MICHAEL C. HEBERT/ SPURLOCK PHOTOGRAPHY, INC.

Dale became "The Dominator" in the International Race of Champions series winning three titles.

MEMORY LANE

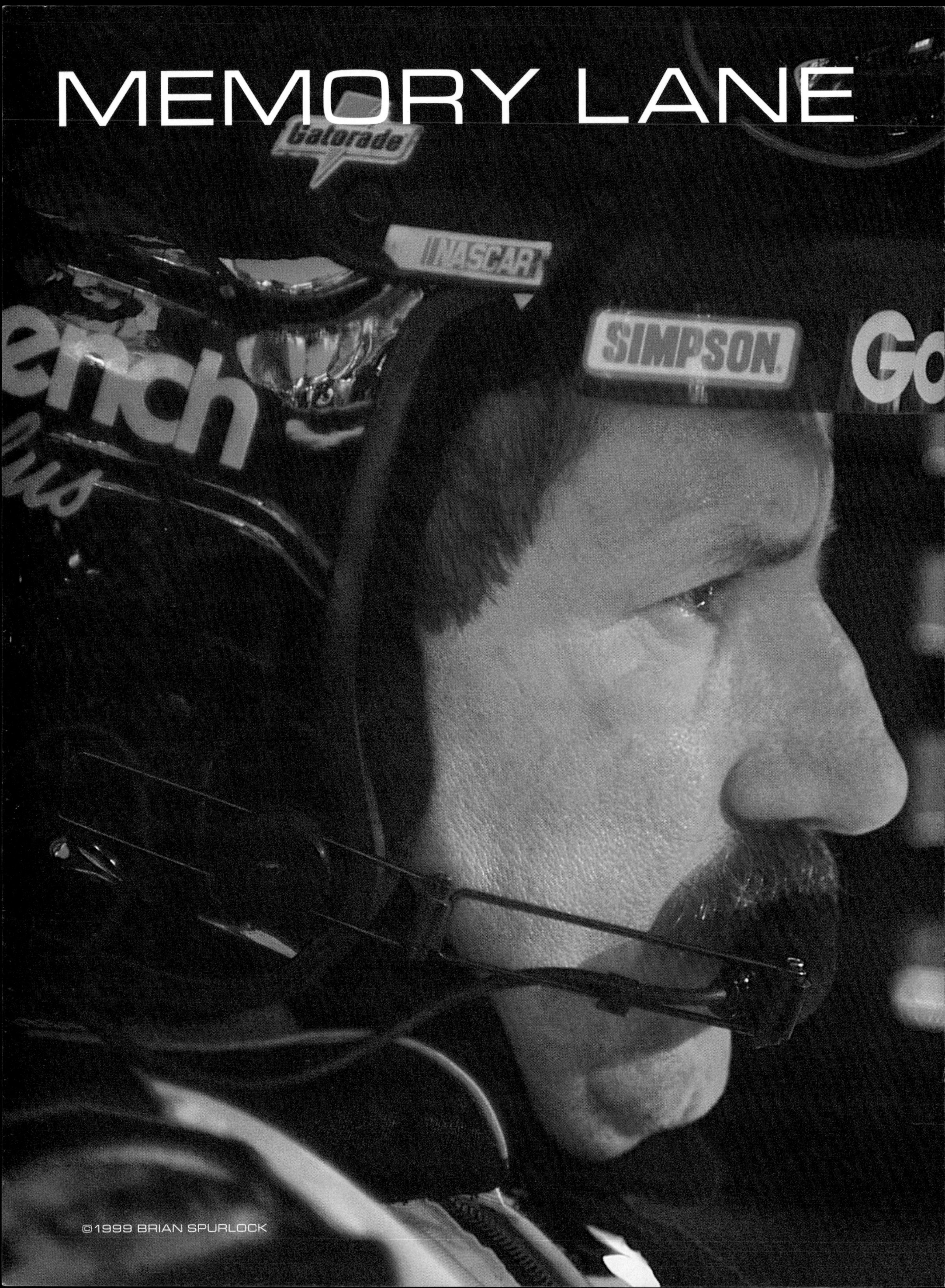

©1999 BRIAN SPURLOCK

Earnhardt was at home behind the wheel of a stock car. He often said that racing was in his blood. "It's who I am."

©1984 JIM BROWN/SPURLOCK PHOTOGRAPHY, INC.

©1987 JAI GIFFIN/SPURLOCK PHOTOGRAPHY, INC.

©1984 JIM BROWN/SPURLOCK PHOTOGRAPHY, INC.

(Top) Earnhardt races Buddy Arrington at Nashville in 1984. (Middle) Pre-race celebrations are underway in 1987 for The Winston. Earnhardt made the infamous "pass in the grass" later that day in a battle with Bill Elliott. (Left) Earnhardt's long-time fishing and hunting buddy, Neil Bonnett celebrates in Victory Lane at Nashville.

Winston Cup Champions Dale Earnhardt, Jeff Gordon and
Bobby Labonte leaving the garage area at Charlotte.

"The Intimidator" arrives
at the office.

Jeff Gordon and Dale Earnhardt
take a break after a long day of
practice at Talladega.

Earnhardt and crew chief Larry McReynolds discuss race setup in the garage area at Indianapolis.

Earnhardt began the 2000 season in
Daytona driving a red car with the
Tazmanian Devil on the hood.

"SWEET HOME ALABAMA"

Earnhardt's 10 wins at Talladega makes him the track's winningest driver. His final career victory came here on October 15, 2000.

Drivers pose for a group photo to celebrate
NASCAR's 50th Anniversary.

Earnhardt accounted for more than $200 million in annual retail sales of licensed NASCAR merchandise. His famous signature is also trademarked.

© 1997 BRIAN SPURLOCK

Dale Earnhardt coming
through the carousel
at Sears Point.

Earnhardt salutes the fans after his
qualifying run at the Brickyard in 1997.

The 3 car barrels into turn 4 at Phoenix.

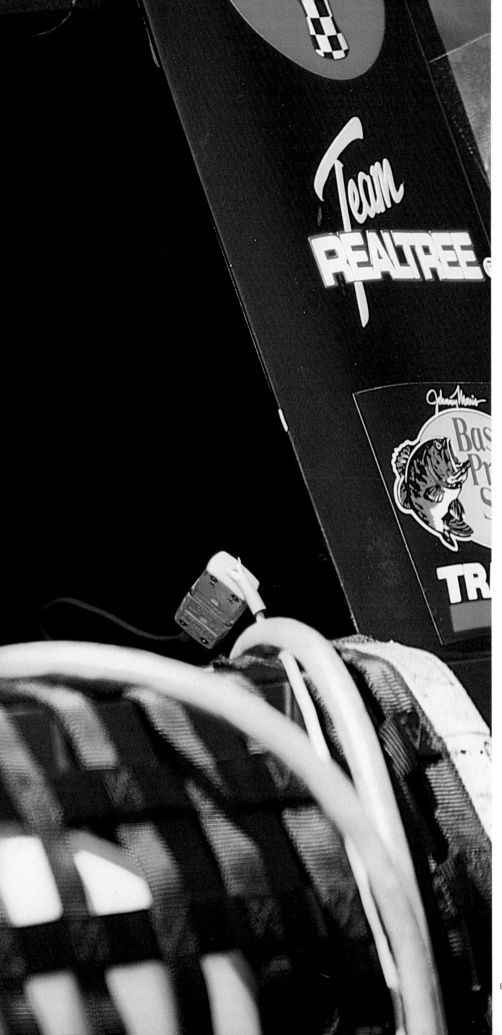

Two of NASCAR's greatest drivers, Darrell Waltrip (left) and Dale Earnhardt (right) share a laugh with their wives as they walk to their cars at Daytona.

Twelve of the world's greatest drivers prepare to do battle in the International Race of Champions at Daytona.

©2000 BRIAN SPURLOCK

Dale's number one fan is
Teresa Earnhardt.

Mark Martin and Dale Earnhardt share
Victory Lane at the Brickyard. Martin won
the IROC race, and Earnhardt took the
series championship.

More than 350,000 fans watch as
Dale Jr. leads Dale Sr. into turn 1 at
the start of the Brickyard 400.

An intimidating sight
at Sears Point.

"The Man in Black" getting the
"Goodwrench Service Treatment."

Winston Cup Champions Jeff Gordon and
Dale Earnhardt, shown here duelling at
Michigan, mutually respected each other
both on and off the track.

Earnhardt gives Wally Dallenbach Jr. some driving tips at Sears Point.

©1997 BRIAN SPURLOCK

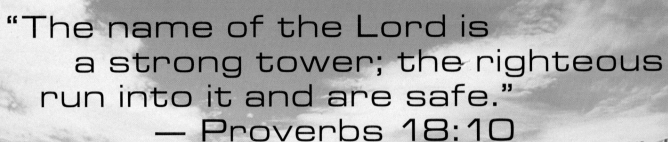

"The name of the Lord is
a strong tower; the righteous
run into it and are safe."
— Proverbs 18:10

Stevie Waltrip taped a Bible verse in Earnhardt's car
before each race. The verse on the dashboard before
the 2001 Daytona 500 was Proverbs 18:10.

©1987 BRIAN SPURLOCK

Winston Cup Champions Dale Earnhardt,
Jeff Gordon and Bobby Labonte leave the
track with checks-in-hand. Ironically,
Earnhardt named his boat "Sunday Money."

In his 20th attempt, Earnhardt won NASCAR's "crown jewel" in 1998.

©1998 SPURLOCK PHOTOGRAPHY, INC.

As the sun set at the Brickyard in 1995, the 3 car was number one.

©1995 BRIAN SPURLOCK

Dale Earnhardt and car owner Richard Childress teamed up to win six Winston Cup Championships. Dale began driving his familiar black 3 car in 1988.

The crew rolls the car to the starting grid at California Speedway.

"The Man in Black" streaks to the finish.

Earnhardt won his only road course event at Sears Point in 1995.

Teresa is all smiles as Dale celebrates his 1995 win at the Brickyard.

FAMILY AFFAIR

Dale Jr. and Dale Sr. swap paint at
Rockingham.

Dale and Teresa share a moment together during the National Anthem at Dover.

The Earnhardts and Childresses celebrate one of Dale's 34 Daytona victories.

Dale Jr. and Dale Sr. battle the crowd after the drivers meeting.

Dale and Teresa, who were married in 1982, were often seen together before the races started.

Michael Waltrip, Dale Earnhardt and their wives take a ride in the pace car as part of the pre-race activities.

The winner's circle is an
Earnhardt family tradition.

Dale Jr. wonders what lies ahead in his Winston Cup future as he prepares for one of his first starts at Michigan.

Taylor Nicole smiles for the cameras as her daddy does his Victory Lane interview.

LIKE FATHER, LIKE SON

Budweiser

SIMPSON.

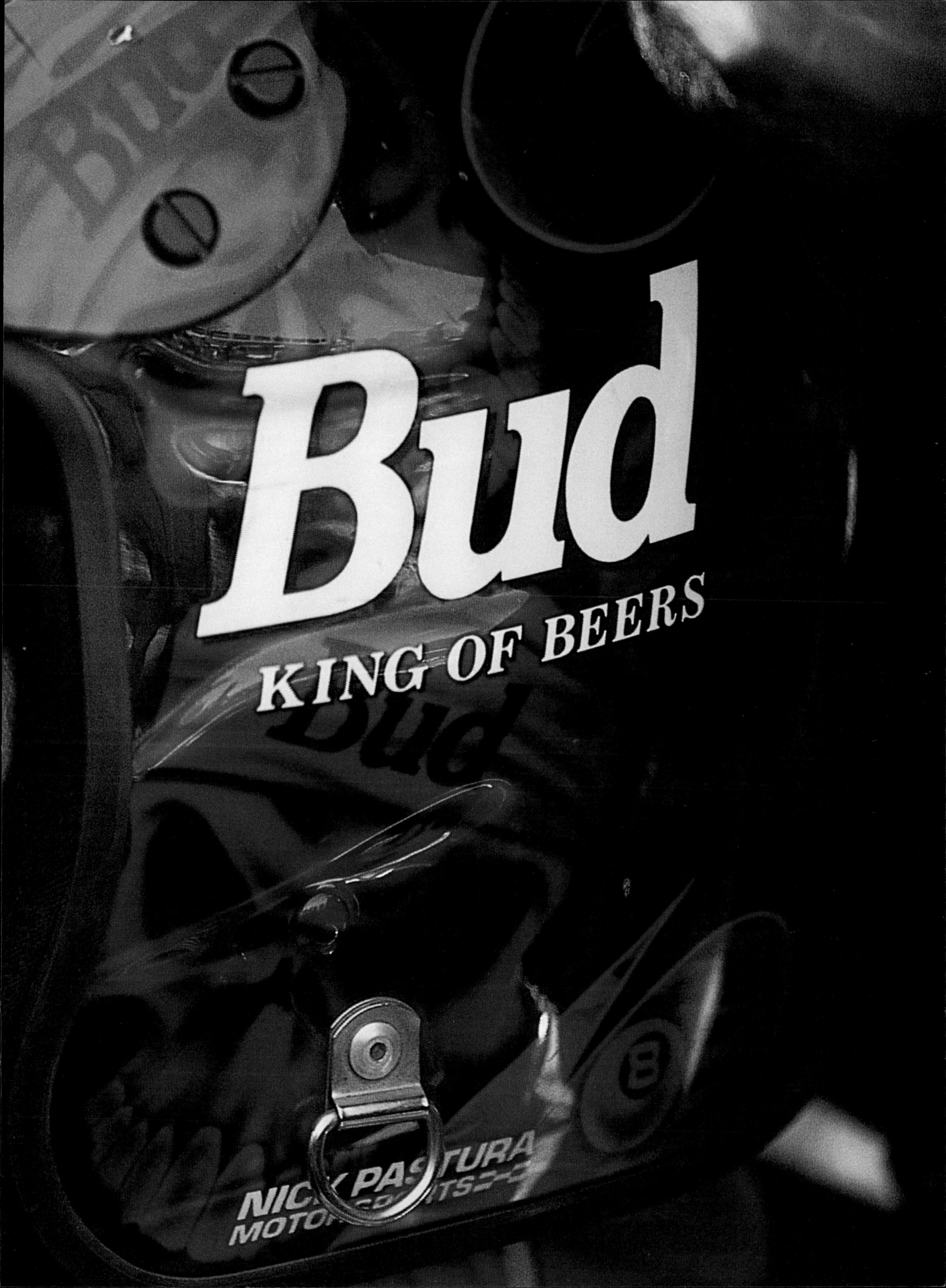
Bud
KING OF BEERS

Dale and Teresa share some laughs before the green flag drops at Phoenix.

Jeff Gordon tries picking up a few family secrets at Michigan.

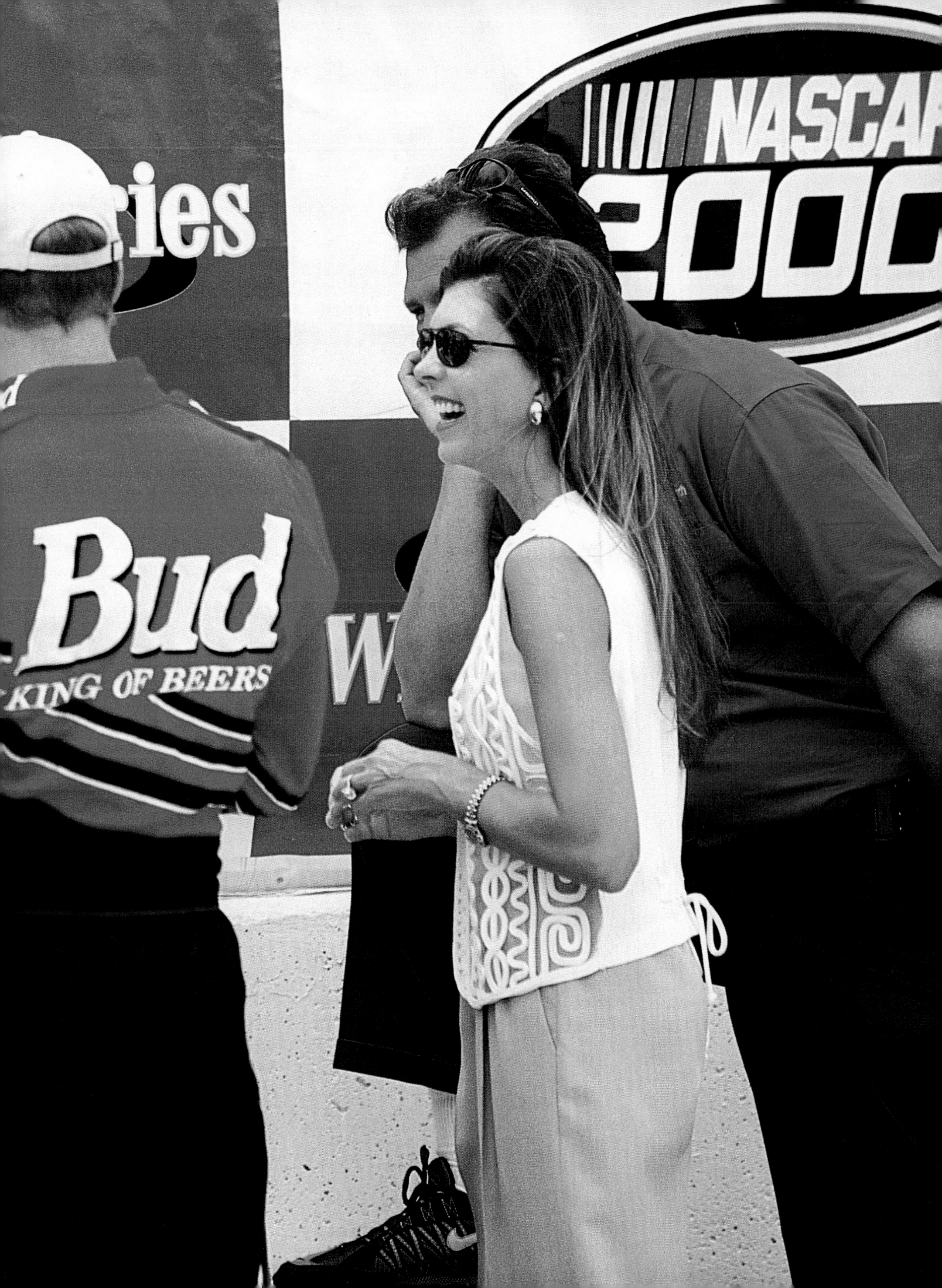
NASCAR
2000
ries
Bud
KING OF BEERS

Earnhardt sported a "no mustache look" in August, 1999 at Indianapolis.

©1999 BRIAN SPURLOCK

© PHOTOS BY SPURLOCK PHOTOGRAPHY, INC.; BRIAN SPURLOCK (8); JOE ROBBINS (3); DON KELLY (1)

FAN FRIENDLY

Always a fan-favorite at Martinsville,
Earnhardt totalled six career
Winston Cup wins at this track.

©2000 BRIAN SPURLOCK

Fans have some fun with cardboard stand-ups at Talladega.
©1997 BRIAN SPURLOCK

A fan-frenzy at Michigan.
©1999 BRIAN SPURLOCK

Dale signs a fan's shirt at Atlanta.

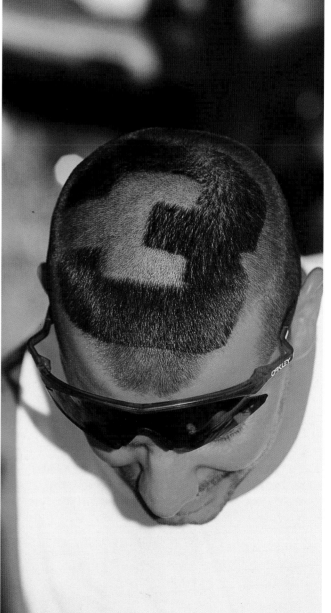

Nothing is too extreme for some
Earnhardt fans.

Earnhardt fans come in all shapes and sizes.
©1997 BRIAN SPURLOCK

Welcome to the Dale Earnhardt Boulevard in the infield at California.
©1997 BRIAN SPURLOCK

Fans anxiously wait to greet the champion outside his hauler.
©1997 BRIAN SPURLOCK

These guys show their true colors.
©1997 BRIAN SPURLOCK

Earnhardt excited fans of all ages.
©1997 BRIAN SPURLOCK

©1999 BRIAN SPURLOCK

"Me and My Chevy Van and that's alright with me."
©1997 BRIAN SPURLOCK

Earnhardt fans dream
about the big race.
©1997 BRIAN SPURLOCK

Everyone fights for a glimpse of Earnhardt.
©1997 BRIAN SPURLOCK

A.J. Foyt and Dale Earnhardt (cutouts) get a fan escort to the
Indianapolis Motor Speedway.
©1996 BRIAN SPURLOCK

Fans wait to see the 3 car leave the garage area.
©2000 BRIAN SPURLOCK

This fan gets up-close and personal with her hero.

©1997 BRIAN SPURLOCK

Fans go to all heights to see The Intimidator.

©1997 BRIAN SPURLOCK

Earnhardt receives his fans' approval at Charlotte.

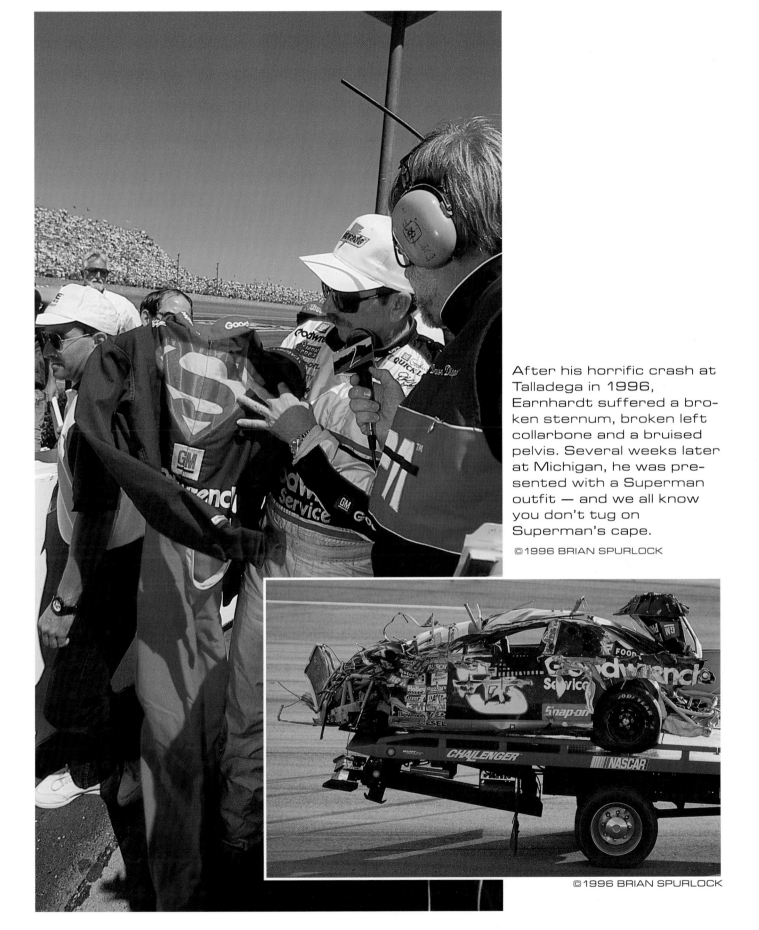

After his horrific crash at Talladega in 1996, Earnhardt suffered a broken sternum, broken left collarbone and a bruised pelvis. Several weeks later at Michigan, he was presented with a Superman outfit — and we all know you don't tug on Superman's cape.

©1996 BRIAN SPURLOCK

©1996 BRIAN SPURLOCK

Feb. 25, 2001 will be remembered as one of the most moving moments in NASCAR as all three crews from Dale Earnhardt, Inc. hold pennants in honor of Dale Earnhardt.

FAREWELL AT ROCKINGHAM

With the flag at half-mast fans mourn.

Steve Park, Dale Jr., and Michael
Waltrip look toward the heavens.

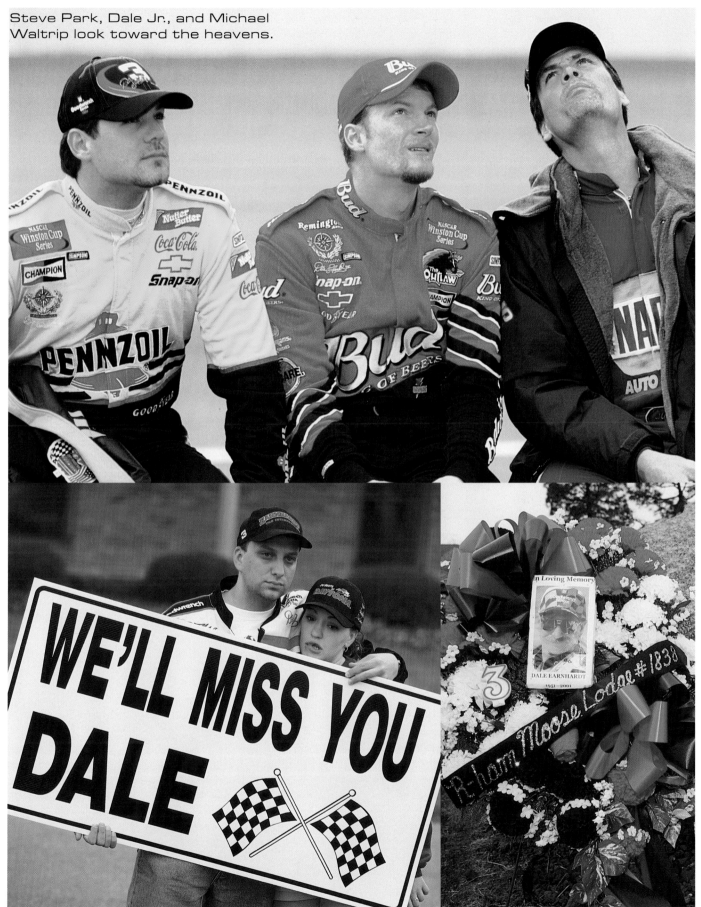

Jeff Gordon

"Brooke and I are deeply saddened by this devastating loss. Not only is it a huge loss for this sport, but a huge loss for me personally. Dale taught me so much and became a great friend."

"Our thoughts and prayers are with Teresa and the entire Earnhardt family."
— *Jeff Gordon*

Kevin Harvick

"Dale Earnhardt was probably the best race car driver there's ever going to be in NASCAR. Nobody will ever replace him and I think we all know that. I would hope you guys don't expect me to replace him, because nobody ever will." — *Kevin Harvick*

"He was a good friend and I'm still in shock. This is a terrible, terrible loss and, for me, it ranks right up there with the death of JFK. Dale was the Michael Jordan of our sport.

"We always thought of Dale as being invincible, so when he didn't climb out of that car after the wreck I knew it was bad.

H.A. "Humpy" Wheeler (middle); Bruton Smith (right)

"I talked to him this morning before the race and he was poised to challenge for an unprecedented eighth championship and was really looking forward to a fantastic season. "I knew Dale's father, Ralph, and I've known Dale since he was a little boy. He had things pretty tough when his father passed away when he was young and I was so proud of the way he turned out and the way he represented our sport.

"Behind that macho facade was a real sensitive individual who did a lot of things for a lot of people and didn't want any publicity in return. He was part of a very loving family and was truly an extraordinary human being. To think he is not around anymore is incomprehensible.

"Right now, we've got to do what we can do to help his family get through this terrible time. Our thoughts and prayers are with his mother, Martha, his wife, Teresa, and his children—Kerry, Dale Jr., Kelley and Taylor Nicole.

"We will never fill the void left by the loss of Dale Earnhardt." — *H.A. "Humpy" Wheeler, President, Lowes Motor Speedway*

"Dale Earnhardt for the next couple of years will make more money in death than when he was alive. It's like Elvis. There is going to be a mad rush; it's already here." — *Bruton Smith, President of Speedway Motorsports, Inc.*

Richard Petty

"We shared a common bond in championships as well as a mutual respect. Our family has raced against his family since this sport began, going back to when my dad and I raced against Ralph Earnhardt." — *Richard Petty*

© PHOTOS BY SPURLOCK PHOTOGRAPHY, INC.; BRIAN SPURLOCK (2); JOE ROBBINS (3); JIM BROWN (3)

Darrell Waltrip

Junior Johnson

Bill France, Jr.

"We always kidded each other about how when we got older and retired, we'd be sitting on the front porch in our rocking chairs watching our kids play out in the yard and comparing careers. He always wanted to outdo me, especially when he first start-ed, because I was kind of a bench-mark at the time. There's a place here (Franklin, TN) that builds these gigantic rocking chairs...Right before I left for Daytona, I went over to check on them, and I was going to get one shipped to his shop because, knowing him the way I do, his rocking chair would have to be bigger than mine. His rocking chair would have to rock faster than mine. He would've been in hog heaven, because his chair would have been so much better than mine." — *Darrell Waltrip*

"When he was just a kid, me and his daddy used to race against each other. He'd play around in the dirt at the racetrack and in the garage. I used to pick on him all the time. He's just a boy that grew up through racing...There ain't no question about it, he was the best. He was the best of any sport." — *Junior Johnson, Hall of Fame Driver and Owner*

"NASCAR has lost its greatest driver ever, and I personally have lost a great friend." — *Bill France, Jr., Chairman of NASCAR*

Dale Jarrett

"As millions of race fans mourn the loss of the man they knew as 'The Intimidator,' the sport and the race that he truly loved has taken from me one of my best friends. I know I should feel fortunate that I had the opportunity to race with, tangle with, sometimes outrun, and like most usually finish behind, the great-est driving talent NASCAR racing has ever seen.

"I am thankful for that opportunity but, more importantly, I am most grateful that I had the chance to know Dale Earnhardt in a way that so many people could only dream of. He was a true friend — someone I could always depend on to give me an honest answer and, at the very least, his opinion. I looked up to him not only because of his driving skills, but because he was so much more to so many people, including me and my family. Kelley and I choose to remember this incredible racer for his caring and giv-ing personality.

"Our thoughts and prayers go out to Teresa and the kids in this time of mourning. But knowing Dale, he would rather this be a celebration of his amazing accomplishments. This, we will do in his honor. Just know, Dale, that we love you and we all are truly going to miss you. Thanks for making our sport what it is today and for being my friend." — *Dale Jarrett*

Max Helton, Motor Racing Outreach Chaplain, prays and consoles Dale Jr.

Dale Earnhardt waves goodbye to the fans and will be forever missed.

I'LL FLY AWAY

"Some glad morning when this life is o'er, I'll fly away,

To a home on God's celestial shore, I'll fly away,

I'll fly away, O'Glory, I'll fly away,

When I die, hallelujah, by and by, I'll fly away."

Fly over at the Daytona 500